WOLVERHAMPTON TRAMS AND BUSES

ALEC BREW

AMBERLEY

Acknowledgements

The basis for the images in this book is a huge collection of slides given me by Francis Washer. Their original attribution is now lost and so I cannot acknowledge the work of the original photographers individually, for which I apologise. A large collection of photographs and insights was also provided by Andy and Ray Simpson, and others came from the Everall family, Simon Dewey and Ned Williams. I also have to acknowledge dipping heavily into Jane Smith's immense book *Accidents: Nineteenth Century Accidents in Wolverhampton*, an indispensable reference work for anyone researching any aspect of the city's history in those years.

First published 2019

Amberley Publishing
The Hill, Stroud
Gloucestershire, GL5 4EP

www.amberley-books.com

Copyright © Alec Brew, 2019

The right of Alec Brew to be identified as the Author of this work has been asserted in accordance with the Copyright, Designs and Patents Act 1988.

ISBN 978 1 4456 8722 3 (print)
ISBN 978 1 4456 8723 0 (ebook)

British Library Cataloguing in Publication Data. A catalogue record for this book is available from the British Library.

Typesetting by Aura Technology and Software Services, India. Printed in the UK.

Contents

Introduction

Wolverhampton has always been something of a pioneer of public transport systems. Within the town the Electric Construction Company and its founding genius, Thomas Parker, were world leaders in electric propulsion, producing the first powered public transport vehicle licenced in London, the first major tramway in Britain, in Blackpool, and locally, the Darlaston to Bloxwich tramway using the overhead collection system.

It was something of a surprise when Wolverhampton itself chose the first and only surface contact system for its own trams, which began to operate in 1902. Bowing to the inevitable, they were switched to overhead contact after the First World War, and then replaced with trolleybuses. For a while the town had the largest trolleybus system in the world – unsurprisingly, as the town hosted two of the world's major trolleybus makers in Guy Motors and Sunbeam.

During the Second World War these two were trusted with the manufacture of the majority of the country's public transport requirements – Sunbeam for trolleybuses and Guy for motor buses, with its Arab becoming a national icon. After these two companies were merged their products filled the streets with Wolverhampton's primrose and apple colours until Guy was swallowed up in the choking tentacles of British Leyland and closed.

Soon after the trolleybuses had all been replaced by motor buses, the town's buses were also swallowed up by the West Midlands Passenger Transport Executive and since then there has been a kaleidoscope of different colours arriving at our bus stops, as different incarnations of the company and the rivals spawned by bus deregulation served Wolverhampton. Things have come full circle as electric propulsion returns to the city's streets with electric hybrid buses, and the trams of the Midland Metro.

It's an old adage that you wait for ages for a bus and then two come along together. This book is filled with the sights which have filled our streets for a century and a half: the happy sight of the next bus just arriving, or the frustrating one of the one just missed.

Horse-Drawn

250 years ago public transport in Wolverhampton was by Shanks's Pony. If you were wealthy enough there might be a horse, or a pony and trap, but if ordinary folk wished to cross the town they walked. In truth that was no great hardship, because the town was so much smaller then, meaning that everything was within walking distance.

Public transport did exist between major towns and cities, by coach and horses, and the main road from London to Holyhead, for the Dublin ferry, passed through Wolverhampton and along the turnpike which stretched from Bilston to Shifnal, with a toll gate in Chapel Ash that was later moved out to Newbridge. In fact the Half Way House at the end of Paget Road was exactly halfway between London and Holyhead, 130 miles in each direction. Much of this route was not good, even on the turnpike sections. Climbing the ridge to Tettenhall involved a winding route around Lower Green and up Old Hill, where a windlass was sited to help wagons and coaches up the steep incline. Even so there were occasions where wagon linkages broke and terrible accidents resulted, often with dire consequences to the horses and people involved.

Thomas Telford was engaged to survey and upgrade the entire route, and the result at Tettenhall was the creation of the Rock and an embankment taking the road to a new bridge over the Staffordshire & Worcestershire Canal. In the centre of Wolverhampton a new road was created from High Green (later called Queen Square) and named Darlington Street, straightening the route which used to go down Cock Street (what later became Victoria Street) and Salop Street. After improvements had been made to the whole of the London to Holyhead route, coaches would take as little as thirty hours to make the journey.

There were other coach services on shorter routes, many with romantic names, such as the Shropshire Hero, the Red Rover, the Royal Dart and the Wonder, which lived up to its name in 1838. On its route from London to Shrewsbury, it beat the train to Birmingham by twenty minutes. The Eclipse Coach ran from Worcester and the Independent from Stafford. Coaching inns in the town vied to serve these coaches as bases for passengers and places to change horses. There were the Angel and the Swan at the top of High Green, the New Inn along Cock Street and, later on, the Star and Garter in Victoria Street. The railways were to end the long-distance coach services before many more years had passed.

Conductors on the coaches had post-horns to warn inns of their imminent arrival, and to have horses ready to change, and to warn people to get out of the way, but accidents still happened. In March 1821 the Bridgnorth Day Coach suffered a broken axletree at Compton, the driver having his leg broken. In October 1824 the Eclipse from Worcester overturned at Stourport because it hit a pile of stone heaped by the side of the road, which was being macadamised. One passenger who had been on top had his thigh broken. In June 1831 Monsieur Bayol, a Frenchman who was travelling to Manchester to see the new Liverpool & Manchester Railway, was riding the Manchester Mail, which arrived at the New Inn in Cock Street. The driver put down the reins to get out his pocket watch in order to tell Monsieur Bayol the time, and the horses bolted. They had reached Craddock's Walk in North Street when one horse collided with a building and died. Monsieur Bayol had jumped off in fright and suffered a broken leg. His companion, Viscount Secqueville, stayed inside the coach and was unhurt. The new railway may have seemed an even more attractive mode of transport after that experience.

Industry, if not passenger travel, was revolutionised by the arrival of the canals in 1792, with the opening of the Staffordshire & Worcestershire connecting the east and west coasts. Its high point was at Compton Lock, from where it ran to the connection with the Birmingham Canal Navigations at Aldersley, rising then through twenty-one locks to Wolverhampton town centre. The town began to change from a rural market town to an industrial centre sucking in people to work in the new metal-bashing industries. New suburbs began to appear, symbolised by the construction of 'Newhampton' in the Whitmore Reans area, and the middle classes began to move out with the leafy edges as they expanded north and west. Walking to work was becoming more difficult, and horse-drawn bus services began to appear.

In 1835 John Doughty started running an omnibus between Birmingham and Wolverhampton, and three years later Rushton's Omnibus service went to Shifnal twice a week. Other more local services were developed, alongside the introduction of hackney cabs. In October 1836 the Regulator Omnibus, with thirteen passengers inside, was approaching the finger-post in Bilston. Witnesses said there were two 'loose characters' on the box with the driver, and he was paying more attention to them than his driving. He dropped the reins and the horses bolted, hitting the finger-post and then running up a coal bank and overturning. All but two of the passengers inside suffered broken bones.

As with modern private bus services, there were sometimes races between companies. In February 1840 the Red Rover coach from Stafford got into one such race with the Queen Omnibus. At full speed they crossed the bridge at Coven and a woman was thrown from the coach. She was run over, dying immediately. The newspapers urged the proprietors to stop such activity.

Different omnibus companies operated the route to Tettenhall and there was often competition to get to the next stop first in order to collect the waiting passengers. On one occasion, on 15 December 1869, one of Mr Atkinson's omnibuses was forced onto the pavement by a rival aggressively forcing in front of him, and one of the horses was injured. The other driver was fined for wilful damage, and sacked by the bus owner.

Of course horses can be very skittish and bolt for no reason. On 8 February 1843 the Grand Junction Omnibus was standing by Low Level station when the horses suddenly started off with no-one on board. They went out to the Wednesfield Road, up Railway Street and down Piper's Row. They turned down Bilston Street and the bus finally overturned near Dudley Street, luckily with little damage.

Horse-drawn trams began to appear from 1860, in London and elsewhere, and they offered a more efficient and safer system. Following the Tramways Act, private companies could apply for Tramways Orders to allow them to lay rails in the public highway.

On 14 December 1878 the Wolverhampton Tramways Company was incorporated with plans to construct lines to Tettenhall, Bilston and Willenhall. The premier route was to be that from Queen Square to Newbridge, terminating at the town boundary, marked by Smestow Brook (and thereby avoiding the steep hill up the Rock). A depot was created on the western side of Darlington Street near the lower end, with another at Newbridge, on the eastern side near the turn into Newhampton Road. The line was 1 mile 5 furlongs (1,100 yards) and the first service was able to run on 1 May 1878, Board of Trade approval having been given after a trial service the day before. The first service left Queen Square at 8 a.m. for the twelve-minute journey to Newbridge on the single-deck tram, which cost 2*d*.

Within six weeks the others routes were opened. The track was standard railway width, 4 feet 8.5 inches. The early cars were single-decker with eighteen to twenty passengers, and an extra horse was needed to pull each one up the incline of Darlington Street. Later on double-decker trams were introduced with open top decks. Horse-drawn buses still operated on routes not served by trams, notably the omnibuses of Sampson Tharme, which served the route to the Rose and Crown on the Penn Road until as late as 1912. Tharme and his brother also operated Hansom cabs in the town.

On one occasion in January 1885, the boy who brought an extra horse out of the Darlington Street stables to help haul a heavily loaded tram up the hill, as was normal, was taking it back to the stables when it was frightened by a piece of paper fluttering in the road, and it backed through the plate glass window of a draper's shop, luckily without injury to horse or boy.

As the tram rails terminated at Newbridge, omnibuses still operated the route to Upper Green Tettenhall, having to negotiate the steep incline of the Rock. On 4 January 1871 the Tettenhall Omnibus, pulled by three horses with fifteen passengers inside and three on top, started up the Hill but there had been snowfall and the road was slippery. The horses could get no purchase with their hooves and the bus started sliding backwards. It slid over the embankment on the corner of Henwood Road, where Majestic Wine is now situated, and fell down into the field below, pulling the horses with it. The three passengers on top all jumped off and were injured, but those inside, and the horses, were nothing more than shaken.

Another horse-tram company, the Dudley, Sedgley & Wolverhampton Tramway, laid standard gauge rails to the Wolverhampton boundary at Fighting Cocks and began running services from 7 May 1883. Because of the hilly nature of this route, three years later they sought Parliamentary permission to operate steam-drawn trams. On 16 January 1886 the first such service left Dudley, running all the way to Snow Hill in Wolverhampton. A Kitson steam locomotive pulled a Starbuck double-decker tram-car which reduced the running time to just forty minutes. Kitson was a Hunslet company which had been making locomotives since 1838; George Starbuck & Co.

was a Birkenhead company, the first to make tram cars outside North America. The company became George F. Milnes & Co. in 1878 when bought out by the company secretary, and in 1899 moved to Hadley in Shropshire.

One Sunday night in November 1886 the last steam tram from Dudley was stopped at Blakenhall. The driver opened the valves and let off the brake, but the tram did not move, so the driver got off to investigate. The tram started moving and knocked him over, but the conductor and passengers were totally unaware that anything was amiss. As the tram approached Snow Hill terminus, still without its driver, the conductor finally suspected that something was awry and applied the brakes, but it was too late. The locomotive ploughed through the end of the rails and swung left on the camber of the road. It cut through the kerbstones, mounted the pavement, tearing up the flagstones, and knocked down a tree, coming to a halt in front of Clarkson's furniture store. Fortunately, no-one was injured.

This was not the case in March 1894 when a Wolverhampton-bound steam tram struck a Dudley-bound omnibus. The horses were injured and one had to be put down, and the driver and one of the passengers were hospitalised. Witnesses stated that the tram driver had been drinking and had set off late as he had been in a pub. He was driving at perhaps twice the permitted 8 mph to make up time. He was fined 20 shillings with £5 costs.

Wolverhampton Tramways had been interested in using steam power from the outset, but there were local objections. In 1880 the company obtained permission from the council to operate a steam locomotive for a six-month trial period. It arrived at Newbridge Depot on Christmas Eve 1880, a fully enclosed locomotive designed to contain the usual emissions. The first trial run was on 4 January, when it hauled a normal horse-drawn tramcar, with forty-six passengers, to Queen Square. It was driven up and down the Darlington Street hill several times, and horses seemed to accept it without alarm.

The official Board of Trade inspection was on 28 January, and apart from concern about the method used to move the locomotive to the other end of the car at the termini, its use was passed. The company was trying its best to mitigate the effects of mechanical locomotion on the refined people of the Tettenhall Road, and used Lancashire coke to power the engine, because it produced minimal smoke and sulphur. Two tramcars were converted to have their brakes operated from the locomotive, and a water tank was installed at Newbridge. By the middle of May the certificate was approved and steam power began to enter revenue-earning service on 18 May.

The trial lasted five and a half months and seems to have been a success, with over 70,000 passengers travelling on the steam tram, which was quicker than the horse-drawn trams but could only maintain the same schedule, having to wait on the passing places for its equine companions. Public opinion preferred its smoother operation, at least those who used it. A huge debate took place within the council and the town, but when the time came to approve a further extension of its use, the council vote was nineteen against and only fourteen for, and the steam locomotive had to be withdrawn.

Wolverhampton Tramways was to come under council ownership in 1899. A committee had been formed in 1896 to consider the town's public transport and it was to recommend that the company should be purchased, and on 6 October 1898 notice was served on the company that the council would be purchasing it for a sum which would eventually be settled as £22,500, with the change-over date being 1 May 1900.

The first municipal tram left Newbridge at 7.40 a.m. on that date. The initial rolling stock consisted of seventeen horse-drawn trams and seventy-five horses, but five of the trams were condemned and three second-hand ones were purchased to replace them. Then, in 1901 twelve further double-deck cars were bought from Liverpool Corporation as an interim measure until the new electric tram system could begin.

As part of its consideration of Wolverhampton's public transport the Tramways Committee had considered the electrification of the system and had recommended the use of overhead wires, but the choice was about to be challenged.

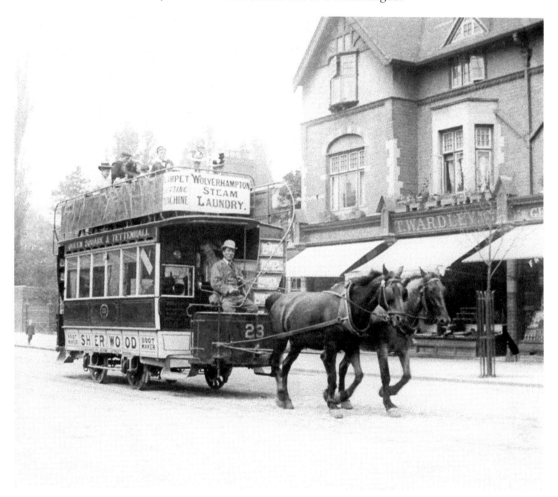

A Wolverhampton Tramways horse-drawn tram entering Chapel Ash on its way from Newbridge. The fact that the driver is not in uniform suggests this is before the network was taken over by the corporation. He appears to be wearing a white bowler hat, which was reserved for drivers on the Tettenhall route. The building in the background is still there, though with new tenants of course. Car No. 23 is now preserved in the Black Country Living Museum.

Wolverhampton Tramways tram No. 24 standing at the Newbridge terminus opposite the northern end of Newbridge Crescent, shortly before the takeover by the corporation in 1900. This was one of four identical trams bought in 1892 and based at the Newbridge Depot. Zebra Grate Polish is not something you see advertised today.

A day out in the early twentieth century involved dressing up in your Sunday best and taking a pony and trap or small coach out into the countryside, and here one such outing is starting from Ye Olde Fieldhouse in Claregate. Note that the man holding the horse is also holding his dog to make sure everyone remains still for the photographer.

The upper part of Dudley Street, between Queen Street and King Street, in the days of horse-drawn traffic, with St Peter's church just visible above. A small bus heads for Queen Square, while a delivery wagon stands outside Freeman's Boots & Shoes. The buildings on the right have all gone.

Colonel Thorneycroft of Tettenhall Towers boards a coach near the top of Old Hill, Tettenhall. Such outfits made the journey from London to Holyhead up Old Hill, until the Rock was cut when the whole length of the main road to Ireland was upgraded after the Act of Union in 1800. The Half Way House at the end of Paget Road is halfway between London and Holyhead, not halfway between Wolverhampton and Tettenhall as many locals believe.

Lorain system tramtracks being laid in 1902 at the junction of Newhampton Road West and Tettenhall Road, those to the left going into town, those to the right going to Tettenhall. The wall in the background is still there.

The staff of the Wolverhampton Tramways Depot at Newbridge, posing in front of one of their horse-drawn trams. The depot was on the eastern side of the Tettenhall Road, near the end of Newhampton Road. What part the three children and the dog played in the tramways' operation is open to conjecture, but they reflect a family atmosphere.

Electric Trams

Within the town there was a pioneer of electric traction, the Electric Construction Company of Bushbury. The first ever electric tram ran on an experimental line between Wolverhampton and Willenhall, with all the power equipment supplied by Elwell-Parker, the predecessor of ECC, which had a factory near Willenhall Road, on Commercial Road. ECC absorbed Elwell-Parker and moved to a larger factory at Bushbury. They went on to supply the first ever large tramway network in Great Britain, in Blackpool, and the overhead electric railway in Liverpool. In 1891 the company supplied an electric, battery-powered omnibus to the London Electric Omnibus Company to ply the route between Charing Cross and Victoria station. It was a double-decker with room for twelve passengers inside and fourteen on the open top deck. It was the first powered public passenger vehicle to be licenced to operate in London, and three fourteen-seat single-deckers were to follow.

Locally, the South Staffordshire Tramways Company sought to electrify the line linking Darlaston and Willenhall, through Walsall to Bloxwich, and chose the overhead collection system, with a new patented connector on the tram poles, which gave extra flexibility and meant the tram did not need to pass directly under the overhead wires. In 1892 ECC was approached to supply all of the electrical equipment for the line, including a power station in Pleck. The trams were double-deckers with provision for eighteen inside and twenty-two passengers on top. The new trams began running on 1 January 1893 and basically ran unchanged until 1922.

In 1896 the British Electric Traction Company was formed to develop and construct electric tramways, particularly throughout the Black Country. It began seeking agreements with the various towns to unify the tramways systems and took a controlling interest in Wolverhampton Tramways, announcing its intention to electrify the system and extend the Tettenhall Line to Wergs Road. In most Black Country towns the council bought out the local tram operators and then leased the lines to BET, but Wolverhampton had different ideas.

When the Wolverhampton Council's Tramways Committee, chaired by Alderman Mander, was formed on 13 July 1896 to consider the future of the town's public transport, it recommended the taking over of the private tramways and it was not surprising, given ECC expertise and local examples, that it also recommended converting them to electric power using the overhead system. When the council took control of Wolverhampton Tramways, the trams and horses were spruced up and the drivers and conductors issued with smart new uniforms. A new era in public transport in Wolverhampton had arrived, with exciting new developments in prospect.

In November 1900 tenders were invited for an electric traction network using overhead collection. At this point a deal of objection was heard to the unsightly nature of the overhead poles and cables, particularly from the good people of Tettenhall Road, and surface contact systems were therefore investigated. Thomas Parker, the electrical genius behind the growth of ECC, had left that company and formed his own, Thomas Parker Ltd, and he advocated a surface contact system using a third rail. Alderman Mander happened to be Chairman of Thomas Parker Ltd. This system was rejected but the council's attention had been drawn to two others. One was the Dolter surface contact system which had been experimentally installed in Paris, and members of the committee travelled there to inspect it. Another system was developed by the Lorain Steel Co. of Ohio, USA. Their system used boxes of studs set between the rails, which were raised magnetically as the tram passed above them, to make contact with a skate beneath the tram. When the tram had passed the studs fell back, and were no longer live. Proponents of the Dolter and Lorain systems were invited to Wolverhampton to explain them to the committee, and after these consultations the Lorain system was chosen.

Concern was expressed at the idea of having 500 volt studs set in the road, and the effect they would have on horses when their iron shoes came into contact. There were cases of horses dropping dead in the street, and there was a widespread belief that they had been electrocuted, but the Lorain company maintained that the studs were not live when a tram was not above them, and that the horses must have dropped dead for other reasons. However reports on the operation of the system soon after it went into use found that the tramways had teams of men testing the studs, and sometimes finding them live, particularly at busy junctions. These were found to be due to defective installation, or short circuits caused by damage in use. For instance from May 1902 to February 1903 a total of 400 damaged boxes were discovered with indicated voltages between 10 and 510 volts. It was also stated that pedestrians had received shocks but no physical damage from stepping on live studs, and that the danger to horses was minimal and therefore acceptable. The same report asserted that overhead live cables were just as potentially dangerous. It is hard to see such a system being allowed in the safety-conscious modern world.

Adoption of this system would mean Wolverhampton's tramways would be totally isolated from neighbouring Black Country towns, which all used the overhead collection system, but this was seen as an advantage in one respect in that it would prevent BET trams 'invading' the borough. The Lorain Company built a trial section of line from the new Municipal Tramways Car Depot, which was built in Cleveland Road, and began operating in January 1902. The company was contracted to build a total of 11.375 miles of track to replace the main horse-drawn routes, and the priority was from the depot, through Queen Square and down Newhampton Road West to Whitmore Reans. This was because the council was promoting a huge Industry and Art Exhibition in West Park which was due to open on 1 May 1902, and it was anxious to show off its new public transport system to visitors, transporting them from the railway stations to the exhibition silently and effortlessly. Day and night working achieved the goal, and though the exhibition turned out to be a financial flop, the new electric trams were a success.

The first three trams, single-deckers numbered 10–12, had Milnes bodies mounted on Lorain-DuPont trucks and entered revenue-earning service on the experimental line to Ettingshall Road from February 1902. The trams were painted green and yellow, the colours that were to be largely retained by the Wolverhampton transport department for all its existence. The double-deck trams numbered 1–9, for the flag-bearing route to West Park, were delivered in January and had ERCTW and Milnes bodies on Lorain-DuPont trucks, entering service from 1 May. A further twelve trams were delivered in July and August, Nos 13–18 with Milnes bodies and Nos 19–24 with ERCTW bodies.

The Whitmore Reans service was extended from Coleman Street to Newbridge on 11 August 1902, allowing Tettenhall passengers to travel this way while the horse-drawn system down the Tettenhall Road through Chapel Ash was replaced, and re-opened with the Lorain system on 12 June. This line was then extended up the Rock to Wrottesley Road on 13 September. Once the Tettenhall route was open, the service through Whitmore Reans was cut back to Leicester Square, but public pressure caused it to be re-opened again as far as Hunter Street. The rails remained down, linking with the Tettenhall line at Newbridge, as this loop remained the only place a tram could be turned round. A spur was put in along Waterloo Road to the Molineux, Wolverhampton Wanderers' football stadium, creating a siding for fans arriving at matches, and this was later extended as the start of the route to Bushbury Lane.

Single-deck tramcars started the route to the Market Place, Willenhall, on 2 April 1904 as far as Coventry Street and then three weeks later to Deans Road. Three extra single-deck trams were bought for this service because the double-deckers could not operate under the railway bridges at Horseley Fields.

In 1903 the Borough Engineer suggested the council investigate the use of the new petrol-powered motor buses that were appearing for use on routes not yet served by trams. A Milnes-Daimler was experimentally tested for five days in 1903, but it was not until 1905 that three Wolseley double-decker buses were purchased and placed on the Penn Fields route, operating between School Street and Stubbs Lane. They had room for sixteen passengers on the top deck and sixteen inside, plus two on the bench seat by the driver. When the tram line on this route was opened in 1909, after the layout of Queen Square was modified and Worcester Street widened, the buses were sold.

Private motor buses also operated in the town. The Great Western Railway began operating three Clarkson 20 hp steam buses from Low Level station to Bridgnorth via Compton on 7 November 1904, and was able to pick up passengers within the town. Just as the residents along the Tettenhall Road often raised objections to new public transport developments, those of the very similar Compton Road were to successfully oppose all electrification of that route, and so neither trams nor the later trolleybuses spoiled the scenery with their rails or overhead wires.

GWR found its Clarkson steam buses, which ran on paraffin under pressure, were unable to manage the Hermitage Hill in Bridgnorth with a full load, and so these were replaced by 20 hp Milnes-Daimler buses on 1 January 1905. Sampson Tharme still operated his horse-drawn buses on the Compton route until 1913, but there were other GWR motor bus services which went along the Compton Road to the villages of Pattingham and Claverley, taking advantage of the council's lack of presence to

Compton. The corporation's transport department finally began operating along Compton Road on 10 February 1914 when it began operating Tilling-Stevens TS3 single-decker motor buses on the route.

Tilling-Stevens was a Maidstone company which began making petrol-electric buses in 1906. They were equipped with a petrol engine which drove a generator that supplied the power to an electric drive – a system that seems very modern in its conception.

The route between Wolverhampton and Dudley remained a bone of contention, as well as the Bilston link to that route at Fighting Cocks. Through journeys could not be made unless trams were fitted with both overhead and surface contact collection systems so they could switch at Wolverhampton's boundary. Local pressure from 1905 caused some of both companies' trams to be so equipped, and Wolverhampton trams with overhead poles began running to Bilston from 9 November 1905, and then Willenhall on 18 April 1906, with the BET trams following suit in October 1906. BET began serving the through route from Dudley to Snow Hill from 15 October 1906, with trams equipped with the Lorain system. Because of the extra 1 ton weight of this, and the fact that the Lorain system used far more current anyway, these dual-equipped trams proved uneconomic, and the through service was reluctantly withdrawn on 10 January 1909. The single-decker tram service to Heath Town started on 22 June 1904, and was extended to New Street, Wednesfield, on 31 October.

Another corporation omnibus service was introduced to serve the new industrial area along Park Lane in September 1911, when two twenty-four-seat Albions were purchased to operate a half-hour service from Queen Square. A plethora of applications by private operators to run omnibuses caused the corporation to decide they would better be operated by its own department and in 1914 four more single-deck Albions were purchased to operate the service to Compton and another route to the Rose and Crown on the Penn Road. These six Albions were given the fleet numbers 1–6.

The start of the First World War brought great difficulties to the town's public transport services with shortages of coal leading to difficulties with electricity supply, and many men volunteering for the armed services, leaving a manpower shortage and causing women to be employed for the first time as conductors. On the other hand there was increasing demand on public transport as industrial output expanded. Mr C. L. Wells sold his private company to the Birmingham & Midland Motor Omnibus Company (Midland Red). The council obtained one of his Albions in 1917, together with two others, and two Tilling-Stevens TS.3s. As these were petrol-electric the War Department considered them unsuitable for service on the Western Front, and so local authorities were able to buy them. Four more were to be bought in 1919.

With the completion of the town's twelve tram routes in 1909, the corporation had forty-nine tram cars. Between then and 1921 another eight were added, all single-deck open-plan four-wheelers. Apart from this purchase of these new trams, by the end of the war the entire tramway system was suffering from neglect and nearing the end of its life. In October 1919 the General Manager submitted a report which recommended the replacement of the Lorain system with the overhead collection system used by every other tramway in the country. The Council accepted his recommendation and the conversion to overhead wires began on the Dudley route from 28 March 1921.

This did not get over the problem that most of the tram rails were worn out and needed replacing, and two thirds of the trams had also neared the end of their useful life. In November 1922 the Tramway Committee visited Birmingham to view the new trolleybus route which had been opened in Neachells. The trolleybus system seemed to offer the advantage of being able to utilise much of the newly installed overhead wiring without the vast expense of replacing all the rails. The visit resulted in the recommendation that the trams should be replaced by trolleybuses, and a new era in Wolverhampton's public transport was about to begin.

A Kitson steam tram-set of Dudley, Sedgley & Wolverhampton Tramways. There were five inside-cylinder Kitson locomotives on the Dudley to Wolverhampton service, hauling double-decker trailer cars built by Starbuck Car & Wagon of Birkenhead, with seats for fifty-four passengers. The upper deck, initially with just a canopy, later had windows fitted, some of which were subsequently removed to reduce wind resistance after high winds blew over a tram on the high ground between Gornal and Sedgley. The steam trams ran from 1886 to 1901, after which electrification of the route took place.

Brand-new Lorain system trams stand in the new Cleveland Road Tramways Depot. No. 19, an ER&TCW car, is ready to head for the Arts and Industrial Exhibition in West Park, while No. 17, a Milnes-built tram, is ready to work the Tettenhall route as far as Newbridge. The large sphere on the tall bracket on the upper deck was to light the upper deck, with another light at the opposite end.

Car No. 61, one of the last trams supplied to Wolverhampton, built by English Electric in 1921, is travelling along Lea Road towards the railway station. With a fully enclosed top deck and driver's position it is better weather-proofed than the early trams.

One of the first Lorain trams passes over the Staffordshire & Worcestershire Canal at Newbridge. This bridge was replaced by a larger concrete bridge in the 1930s which features a bus stop layby. The coal yard to the right was then moved beyond the other bridge over the canal, from which this photograph was taken.

A Lorain tram descends Snow Hill, with the Agricultural Hall behind the statue of Sir Pelham Villiers to the left. The hall was replaced by the Gaumont Cinema, and then by Wilkinson's store. The old horse-drawn and steam-powered trams used to terminate here. The statue of Wolverhampton's longest serving MP is now in West Park.

A Walsall Tramways car about to set out for Bloxwich, possibly from Willenhall. The neatly uniformed driver and conductor are standing patiently for the photographer, but the solitary passenger is looking impatient for his journey to begin.

The single-decker tram about to run between Kingswinford and Dudley, a service which last ran on 31 December 1925 following increasing pressure from motor buses and falling passenger numbers. The tram is standing outside the Cross Hotel. The service was opened by the Dudley & Storubridge Tramways Company, later part of the British Electric Traction Company.

The interior of the Wolverhampton Tramways Depot in Cleveland Road, showing inspection pits beneath two of the lines and a pair of single-decker motor buses in the background. The Cleveland Road Depot opened in 1902 and was finally demolished in 2017.

A Milnes-built Lorain system tram, No. 16 stands at the Bushbury terminus. This route started in 1904 as an extension to the short branch to Molineux Stadium. Two Tramways employees stand on the pavement watching, one of them an Inspector. The toast-rack reversible seat backs can be seen on the upper deck.

Two single-decker trams operate in the centre of Heath Town on the Wednesfield route. Both Heath Town and Wednesfield were separate boroughs at the time. It is interesting to note that the trams are still running despite snow on the ground. Only single-decker trams could operate on this route until the road under the rail bridges at the start of the Wednesfield Road was lowered.

A British Electric Traction double-deck tram passes a single-decker in the centre of Dudley while on its way to Kingswinford, which was one of the western termini of the system. From there it was possible to travel by tram throughout the Black Country and Birmingham, changing trams in town centres.

Wolverhampton Municipal Power Station in Commercial Road, which provided the power for the town's trams and later trolleybuses. It initially had two wooden cooling towers, later replaced by a single concrete one. Coal came in by canal, at the rear, and this was always a good spot for local children to swim as it was kept warm by the power station discharge. The power hall of the station is still standing.

A Wolverhampton Corporation single-decker, converted post-war to overhead collection, is seen outside the Cleveland Road Tramways Depot. It is about to operate on the Willenhall route, where single-deckers were still required because of the low railway bridge in Horseley Fields.

A UEC-built tram delivered in 1908, No. 44 is seen on a special service. Unusually, this was fitted with Mountain & Gibson 21EM trolleys – one of only six trams to be so equipped (Nos 44–49). It was later fitted with a top cover and a vestibule to protect the driver from the weather. The last of these six trams, No. 49, is now preserved in working order in the Black Country Living Museum.

A Dudley & Stourbridge tram slowly works its way through Dudley Market Place, a task which must have been something of a nightmare for the driver.

A Walsall Corporation double-decker stands outside the Kings Arms Hotel in Bloxwich High Street, ready to start its journey back across town. The route to Bloxwich was so popular that the lines were doubled in 1921.

An early Walsall tram passes through The Bridge with the statue of 'Sister Dora' in the background. Dorothy Pattinson, to give her real name, worked as a nurse in Walsall from 1864 until just before her death in 1878. Her tireless work helping the sick and injured of the town has left a legacy which extends well beyond her statue.

A twenty-four-seat Albion single-decker bus, one of six bought pre-war to serve the growing new estates of Fallings Park and Bushbury, stands awaiting passengers on Bushbury Road.

Trams passing through The Bridge in Walsall, the heart of the Walsall tramway system. The clock says it is 3.20 p.m. The statue of Sister Dora is to the right in front of the George Hotel. In 1916, Zeppelin L21 dropped bombs on Walsall and one hit a tram car in Bradford Street. The Mayoress, Mrs Mary Slater, was killed.

A Lorain tram passes through Chapel Ash on its way into town from Tettenhall, having just passed Charles Clark's showrooms, then a 'Carriage and Motor Works' and later a car showroom, until it moved just round the corner into Merridale Road in the 1970s.

During the First World War, a large number of women became tram conductors for the first time in order to replace the men who had gone off to war, This is the license of Ethel Jones of Poole Street, issued on 9 November 1917. It was the 463rd such license issued.

Three Walsall trams, two heading to Pleck, stand by Sister Dora's statue at The Bridge in Walsall. Walsall tram services began to be closed in 1928, and the final Walsall tram ran on 30 September 1930.

A tram operating during the First World War, on the Wednesfield route, when women were recruited as conductors (the ubiquitous 'clippie'). This is Milnes-built tram No. 8, showing signs of long service.

A Dudley & Stourbridge Tram, No. 118, about to start the journey from Stourbridge to New Inns in Lye. It is interesting to think how quickly an integrated tram service was built right throughout Birmingham and the Black Country, all up and running in about ten years, compared to the length of time it has taken the Midland Metro to build and then extend just one line.

A BET double-decker tram built by ER&TCW runs through the Bull Ring in Sedgley on its way from Dudley to Wolverhampton.

A Lorain tram passes through Queen Square with another outside the much-missed Queen's Arcade entrance to the right and the Empire Palace Theatre to the left.

Two Dudley & Stourbridge single-deckers stand waiting below Castle Hill in Dudley, with Dudley Opera House behind them.

A Walsall Corporation double-decker tram, No. 43. This was a post-war-supplied tram, built by the Brush Electrical Company.

A Birmingham Corporation tram, No. 23, in the centre of Dudley below Castle Hill, about to start the journey to Handsworth. This tram had a roof put on the upper deck in 1911. From this spot trams could be taken to Birmingham, Wolverhampton, Stourbridge and throughout Dudley.

A Wolseley double-deck motor bus, one of three bought in 1905 to operate the Penn Fields service, until Worcester Street could be widened and the tram tracks could be laid. It carried eighteen passengers on top, and eighteen inside, two of them seated on the bench by the driver. Symbolically, it is overtaking a horse-drawn bus.

A Clarkson single-decker 20 hp steam-powered bus, one of three bought by the Great Western Railway to operate the Low Level station to Bridgnorth service. It used paraffin under pressure as the fuel. The buses went into service in November 1904, but were withdrawn the following month when they had difficulty climbing the Hermitage Hill out of Bridgnorth. They were sent to Somerset and replaced by Milnes-Daimler motor buses.

A GWR Milnes-Daimler standing outside the Wheel o'Worfield public house on the Bridgnorth road. This one was registered DA 117 in Wolverhampton and introduced in 1905. The pub is now much larger and the road has been widened due to the building on the other side being knocked down. The GWR had designs on connecting Wolverhampton to Bridgnorth and bought the railway company promoted for that route, building the line from Low Level through Tettenhall to Stourbridge Junction, which was opened in 1925. The branch from Wombourne through Halfpenny Green to Bridgnorth was never built, and buses continued to operate the service instead.

Car No. 49 of the Kinver Light Railway, stopped en route for a photograph. This is one of three open-sided trams, which featured closed cabins for twelve people at each end and toast-rack style seating in the centre for thirty-six more. The KLR proved very popular for days out. On Good Friday 1901, 14,000 people made the journey despite pouring rain all day.

A KLR tram outside the Ambelcote Depot of BET, with Dudley & Stourbridge single-deckers inside. People from all over Birmingham and the Black Country could travel by tram out into the countryside at Kinver via the centre of Dudley and Ambelcote.

Trolleybuses

The route chosen to trial the new trolleybuses was the one through Heath Town to Wednesfield. Because of the low bridges under the railway at the start of the route, only single-deckers could be used, and Tilling-Stevens was asked to supply them. It adapted its standard petrol-electric design, the TS3, by replacing the petrol motor with electrical components supplied by BTH of Bath, and six of the resulting Tilling-Stevens TS6 forty-seat vehicles were purchased, each with a central passenger door in a body which was supplied by Christopher Dodson, a London coachbuilding firm based in Willesden.

Trams ceased running on 23 July 1923 and motor buses were substituted while the necessary changes were made. The new trolleybuses began operations on 29 October and were trialled for one year. The trial was such a success that the decision was made to replace all the town's trams with trolleybuses, and the next line to be converted was that to Bushbury, though the route was altered from going via Waterloo Road to via North Street, and was then extended to The Vine public house at Fordhouses. Turning circles were installed at Bushbury Lane, the new Goodyear factory and at the terminus at The Vine. One of the advantages of trolleybuses was the ease with which services could be extended or changed. As on the Wednesfield route, hired motor buses kept the route going while the changes were made, and eight more Tilling-Stevens TS6 trolleybuses were purchased.

The route to Dudley still presented complications, not least because various sections outside Wolverhampton's boundary were owned by more than one local authority. Long negotiations finally led to the corporation purchasing the rights to the entire route, as well as BET's Sedgley Depot. This came with six tramcars and sixty-six employees, which allowed a new trolleybus service to be built and to operate along the entire route. It was opened in four stages starting with Snow Hill to Fighting Cocks on 26 October 1925, and finally reaching Dudley 8 July 1927.

The other tram routes – to Whitmore Reans, Tettenhall, Penn Fields, Bilston and Willenhall – followed in turn. Further Tillings-Stevens TS6 trolleybuses were acquired until the total had reached thirty two, the last arriving on 17 February 1926, but subsequent trolleybuses were to be made in Wolverhampton.

Guy Motors of Park Lane supplied its first trolleybus to the corporation on 1 December 1926, a Guy BTX60 with a double-deck sixty-one-seat Dodson body and an open staircase at the rear. It was the first three-axle trolleybus in the world, and like all Guy trolleybuses featured regenerative braking.

Sidney Guy had resigned his position as Works Manager of the Sunbeam Motor Car Co. in 1913 and set up his own company making commercial vehicles – 30 cwt lorries to begin with. One of these was fitted with a combined bus/mail carrier body for use in Scotland, but this remained the company's only bus until after the First World War. A version of this was produced after the war equipped as a charabanc or a bus, but basically using the same straight framed chassis as Guy lorries. These continued to be sold until 1931.

Guy had begun building a dropped-frame chassis specifically for motor bus applications in 1924, with three different wheelbases. In 1926 a revolutionary three-axle chassis was produced, the BX with a Guy four-cylinder engine, or the BKX with a Knight six-cylinder, both with normal control. Then the following year forward control versions of each were offered.

In 1926 Guy adapted these chassis for electric power, initially with Rees-Stevens electrical equipment, but soon with its own design, which it had built by the Electric Construction Co. (ECC) one quarter of a mile away. The BTX was to be one of four different size trolleybuses offered to the growing world market, the others being the BT32 two-axle thirty-five-seat single-decker, the BT48 three-axle fifty-four-seat double-decker and the BTX66, which was a foot longer than the BTX60 and able to take a single or double-deck body.

The motor buses continued to be built and developed alongside the trolleybuses, and in 1928 Guy acquired the Star Motor Car Company of Walsall Street, and its twenty-seat bus the Star Flyer, which continued to be produced until 1932 at the Fallings Park factory. It was superseded by the Guy Wolf, which had a fourteen to twenty-seat body powered by a Meadows 20 hp petrol engine, from the Henry Meadows factory next door to Guy. This engine also powered the slightly larger Guy Vixen, and both Wolf and Vixen were offered with an alternate Meadows diesel engine from 1934.

With the Wolverhampton fleet number 33, the new Guy BTX trolleybus entered service on the Sedgley route, and fifteen more were to follow in 1927, as well as a further eight the following year.

Avoiding the complications which had always inflicted the Wolverhampton to Dudley route, both Wolverhampton and Walsall councils sought complimentary Parliamentary powers to build and operate a through service between the two towns via Willenhall, with a turning circle there, for short services. Walsall delayed giving up its trams, which served as far as Willenhall until 1931, when the road under the bridges in Horseley Fields had been lowered to allow double-deckers to be used on the route, and after that the blue Walsall trolleybuses were to be seen in Wolverhampton, with the green and yellow Wolverhampton buses travelling the whole route to Walsall.

Penn Fields and then Tettenhall was converted, with the Tettenhall service terminating at Wrottesley Road, beginning on 2 January 1928. The Whitmore Reans service followed, with a circular route in the suburb going either clockwise or anti-clockwise around Court Road and Hordern Road. This left trams operating on just the Bilston route, where some of the line was owned by BET. Parliamentary approval for the purchase of this was not finalised until 3 August 1928, at which point it took over the Bilston Depot with fifteen trams. The final Wolverhampton Corporation tram service had taken place on 26 August, but the takeover of the Bilston service meant that it became a tram operator again for a short period, until 25 November.

The conversion of the town's public transport system to trolleybus and motor bus services brought about a re-designation of the route numbering, with new numbering and destination boxes, equipped with roller blinds, on all vehicles. Tettenhall remained route 1, and the full list was as follows:

1. Tettenhall
2. Whitmore Reans via Court Road
2a. Whitmore Reans via Hordern Road
3. Bushbury
3a. Fordhouses
4. Penn Fields
5. Willenhall
5a. Walsall
6. Heath Town
6a. Wednesfield
7. Bilston
7a. Darlaston
8. Fighting Cocks
8a. Sedgley
8b. Dudley
9. Amos Lane
9a. Bushbury Hill
9b. Low Hill
11. Mount Road
11a. Penn
12. Finchfield via Bradmore
13. Merry Hill
24. Willenhall to Bilston
25. Willenhall to Fighting Cocks

Wolverhampton now had the largest trolleybus network in the world, one which eventually stretched 46 miles. By 1933 there were fifty-nine Guy BTX trolleybuses in service, but by then the town had a second major manufacturer. The Sunbeam Motor Car Company had not dabbled in commercial vehicles to any great extent, but the depression in the private car market caused it to look at the new 'sunrise' industry of trolleybuses as there was an explosion in their adoption by cities across the world – a market Guy was exploiting. They had produced the Sunbeam Sikh three-axle and Sunbeam Pathan two-axle single-deck motor buses in 1928, and sales had been disappointing – possibly the use of petrol engines in an era when diesels were becoming the norm had something to do with it. This was ironic as the Sunbeam Pathan aero-engine, developed at this time, was a diesel, a version of the petrol-powered Dyak. Sunbeam saw a future for diesel aero-engines which failed to materialise, but did not foresee a future for diesel buses. The prototype Pathan and three others were brought into service by Wolverhampton in 1929 and used primarily on the Bridgnorth route, but only sixteen others were built.

Sunbeam therefore switched its attention to electric power. The first Sunbeam MS2 three-axle double-decker with Weyman bodywork was trialled by the corporation from July 1931, and was eventually accepted on charge the following year as fleet number 95, alongside three others, fleet numbers 92–94. Henceforth the corporation split its orders between the town's two manufacturers, and representatives of transport departments across the world travelled to Wolverhampton to examine the network and the products of the two companies.

The Sunbeam buses were beautifully made and also featured regenerative braking, which could cause its own problems when the trolleybus system was quiet. Harsh braking put so much current back into the system that the polarity of the mercury arc rectifier could be reversed, bringing everything to a standstill.

Wolverhampton was almost forced to operate a mixed fleet, as to favour one or other of the town's bus makers may well have penalised the others in the eyes of other potential customers. Trolleybus orders were therefore more or less equally split between Sunbeam and Guy, and single-deck motor bus orders included small batches from each of the town's manufacturers – AJS, Guy and Sunbeam – until Guy came to dominate the motor bus orders when its Arab single/double-decker appeared.

As well as the replacement of the trams by trolley-buses, Wolverhampton's motor bus routes were also expanded and developed through the 1920s. The GWR route to Bridgnorth was bought in 1923, and then services to the villages north of the town, like Halfpenny Green, Pattingham, Trysull, Tettenhall Wood, The Wergs, Beckbury, Tong and Wombourne. At the same time a fare agreement was reached with Midland Red to protect fares on common routes. The corporation also bought its first Guy single-decker buses with half a dozen between 1925 and 1926. In 1926 the first double-decker motor bus was purchased since the days of the Wolseleys before the First World War, a Guy CX fifty-five-seater with a Dodson body. This proved so successful that by 1929 another twenty-two Guy CX normal control buses had entered service in the town, together with one FCX forward control version. A sixty-six-seat petrol-electric Tillings-Stevens TS15A was also tried, but was not so successful.

AJS was another Wolverhampton vehicle manufacturer which was in financial difficulties during the Depression and turned to commercial vehicle manufacture as a solution. They produced the twenty-seat Pilot bus in February 1928 and the larger thirty-seat Commodore in 1931. Wolverhampton Corporation bought the prototype Commodore and operated it for seven years. Sadly, although seventy others were sold it was not enough to save AJS, which went into liquidation late in 1931.

Sunbeam was also to go into receivership in 1935 and was sold to Rootes Securities, who closed the car manufacturing side of the business. However, it not only kept the trolleybus line going, but also moved its Karrier trolleybus division to Sunbeam's Moorfield Works from its home in Huddersfield. Five Sunbeam MS3 low chassis double-deckers and four MF1 single-deckers had followed the first Sunbeams into service.

Through the 1930s Wolverhampton's trolleybus routes were adapted and expanded, with new areas served, like Bushbury Hill, Bradmore and more cross-town routes. Victoria Square became the main town hub; essentially a large turning circle, routes radiated outwards, with passenger loading from the central island. In 1936 three more Sunbeam MF1 single-deck trolleybuses were purchased, and by the middle of 1937 the last of the Tilling-Stevens single-deckers was retired, most of the roads under low railway bridges in the town having been lowered to accommodate double-deckers.

The historic first Guy BTX, fleet number 33, was sold back to Guy in 1936 with the intention of it appearing in a new museum, but pressure on space and finances meant this never happened and it was eventually scrapped.

From 1934 Wolverhampton began buying Daimler COG5 buses, and by the outbreak of war had fourteen single-deckers and no less than forty-eight double-deckers in service. They also bought three of the first Guy Arab I double-deckers. By the outbreak of the Second World War, Wolverhampton also had seventy-four Guy trolleybuses in service and fifty Sunbeams.

Guy had revealed the Arab chassis in 1933, the first to be designed for the Gardner diesel engine. L. Gardner & Sons was an engine manufacturer of long standing based in Hulme, Manchester. The Arab was produced in FD32 or FD35, depending on seating capacity as a single-decker, and as the FD48 double-decker, with either the Gardner 4LW, 5LW or 6LW engines. Guy also produced the smaller Wolf CF14 and CF20 models, and then the Vixen 24 and 26. Despite the reliability that the Arab was to demonstrate, there proved to be few customers before the war.

As at the start of the First World War, numbers of transport department staff, drivers and conductors volunteered for the Armed Services, and women were recruited to make up the difference. For a while services were cut back to save electricity, particularly late in the evening. Six buses and ten trolleybuses were on order at the start of the war, but the government forced the cancellation of the order. The corporation was able to hire twelve trolleybuses from Bournemouth, which, like most seaside towns, had surplus capacity during the war due to little tourism, and the twelve yellow Sunbeams were towed back to their place of manufacture. Sunbeam was the only manufacturer permitted to keep making trolleybuses, these being seen as essential for munitions workers to get to work. They made just one standard model: the Sunbeam/Karrier W4. In 1940 the council was permitted to buy ten new Sunbeams, and twenty new motor buses the following year as the town's fleet fell into a poor state of maintenance.

In the same way that Sunbeam was allowed to make a basic, standard trolleybus, the government permitted Guy Motors to build a standard, simplified version of its pre-war Arab with a Gardner diesel engine, and 500 were ordered to provide for the requirements of operators all over the country. This was to be the making of the Arab, which led to it becoming one of the most common buses in the UK. A further 1,500 of the slightly modified Arab Mk II were built by the end of the war, and were supplied with bodies from various manufacturers to operators all over the country. Both the Sunbeam W4 and the Arab were usually supplied in a basic grey colour scheme. With Daimler production having been moved to the old Courtauld's factory on Hordern Road because its Coventry plant had been bombed out, a significant proportion of Great Britain's public transport vehicles were made in Wolverhampton.

Wolverhampton had acquired sixty-nine trolley poles along with the buses from Bournemouth, with the intention of extending the Fordhouses route to the Boulton Paul

Aircraft factory at the end of Wobaston Road. Here a bus turning circle was completed outside the factory, where as many as 5,000 people worked during the war. Buses from the other direction had to stop on the Bilbrook side of the canal as the bridge was not strong enough at the time. The route was never extended as there was official concern that the flashes of the overhead wires at night might attract the Luftwaffe. A dummy Boulton Paul factory was also built a mile further along the canal, out in the countryside, with a prominent bus turning circle alongside, almost like an aiming point, but the Germans were not fooled. Their bombing maps showed both the real and the dummy factory and only the real thing was ever attacked, though the solitary raider missed his target.

Wolverhampton's public transport was never disrupted by German bombing as much as was the case in many other cities, but on the night of 31 July 1942 a bomber did drop a load of bombs on the Willenhall Road and a very large one blew a huge crater just to the Willenhall side of Coventry Street. For a while passengers from Willenhall had to alight on one side of the crater and walk round to catch another trolleybus on the other side. This was a blessing in disguise for the people of Coventry Street, who previously had to stand all the way into town on the crowded buses but could now claim a seat on the empty buses waiting on the Wolverhampton side.

Bus driving in the war held great difficulties. The buses were fitted with hooded headlights which have little forward vision, and of course there were no street lights or light from adjacent buildings. It was so dark that one passenger alighting in Queen Street on her way to the night shift at Fischer Bearings lost her shoe and could not find it, even feeling around with her stockinged foot in the gutter.

By the end of the war much of the town's fleet of buses was in need of refurbishment or replacement. The Bournemouth trolleybuses were returned after the war, though not immediately, and new ones were ordered from Sunbeam and Guy. Approval was given for the delivery of fifty-two new trolleybuses and thirty new motor buses. In the immediate post-war years a total of eighty-six Sunbeam F4 and fifty Guy BT trolleybuses, all with Park Royal bodies, went into service, the last arriving in May 1950. In addition a total of fifty-four trolleybuses were totally re-bodied and put back into service.

In 1948 Rootes Securities sold its Sunbeam trolleybus business to Guy who moved production across town to a new extension at the Park Lane factory, and thus became the largest trolleybus manufacturer in the world, continuing to make both Sunbeam and Guy-badged trolleybuses. There was a tremendous market for buses after the war as towns and cities were finally able to replace their tired equipment.

A total of forty-two new Daimler double-decker motor buses were put into service by 1950, as well as five more Arab IIs, and fifty of the new post-war Arab IIIs, which featured a greater use of aluminium alloys to reduce weight and were just about recognisable externally by a bonnet that was 4 inches lower. The Arab was still mostly sold with the Gardner diesel engine, though the alternative Meadows 6DC630 diesel was offered from 1948 to 1951, but this had few takers. The Henry Meadows factory was next door to Guy on Park Lane, Wolverhampton.

In addition the town's entire electricity overhead supply was refurbished and rationalised, and even the council's power station in Commercial Road received new generating equipment.

On 22 May 1946 a Sunbeam MF2 trolleybus on its way back from Tettenhall suffered a famous but bizarre accident. As it reached the embankment at the bottom of the Rock it suddenly veered left and through the railings above St Michael's School. It plunged down the slope and was only halted when it hit a sapling. The conductor and the driver and the ten passengers were unhurt as they clambered out. Then there was the problem of getting it back on the road. The next day a traction engine was summoned from the depot of Pat Collins Fairs in Walsall, and that proved insufficient, so a second was sent for, from the current site of the fair. The combination of these two monsters finally managed to drag the almost undamaged trolleybus back on to the road, with a large audience, including children in the school below. This accident almost echoed that of the horse-drawn bus nearly seventy years earlier, except that it was on the other side of the embankment.

This particular trolleybus, 295, obviously had something of a jinx as it overturned later the same year, this time at Bradmore on 22 November, though again with no significant injuries. 295 was again returned to service until sold to Belfast Corporation in 1952.

Deliveries of the new buses was delayed by shortage of materials, and oftentimes Don Everall coaches had to be hired to make up the shortfall, as many as twenty-six at a time. Don Everall was the town's premier coach operator. Don himself started the company in the 1920s when coaches were known as charabancs. The company expanded with depots across the Black Country, the main one being located off the Bilston Road. It also ran travel shops, holiday camps and car dealerships. In the 1950s Don Everall took over the management of Wolverhampton Airport and then began its own airline, Don Everall Aviation Ltd, flying services mainly from Birmingham Airport. The company was also well known for supplying the Wolverhampton Wanderers FC team coach, and fleets of coaches to take fans to away games, and Don was a director of the club.

No new trolleybuses were bought after 1950, with the last ninety-nine being a mixture of the very similar Guy BT and Sunbeam F4 models, by now all 8 feet wide, surpassing the previous 7-foot 6-inch width. After 1951 there was a programme of re-bodying the wartime utility-bodied buses. The late 1950s saw the trolleybus system working at its maximum, but the corporation was prevented from expanding by government policy, which led to difficulties with sufficient capacity during the fuel crisis resulting from the Suez blockade. The electricity supply was also switched from the council's own Commercial Road power station to the National Grid, and there were cost rises.

At the start of the 1950s motor buses represented only a third of the town's bus fleet, but at the end there was almost parity. After two major reviews of the future of the town's public transport, the committee held a third in 1961 and considered a report by the general manager that the trolleybuses should be withdrawn from service as their working life ended and replaced by motor buses. The reasons cited were a lack of flexibility and cost, and the report is claimed to have been heavily biased. Nevertheless, the council duly approved this in March.

The first route to be turned over to diesel operation had been the 32 to Oxbarn Avenue, which had preceded this decision, and all the others followed one by one.

A total of 150 Guy Arabs IVs were ordered to replace the trolleybuses, to be delivered over a number of years.

At Guy Motors all bodywork production had ceased in 1953, and after that outside coachbuilders made all the bodies. At the same time the lease on the old Sunbeam Works expired and Sunbeam trolleybus production was moved to Fallings Park. In 1951 Birmingham requested an upgraded Arab, with a more modern front with faired-in radiator, and a Gardner 6LW engine with pre-selector gearbox. This emerged as the Arab IV, which became the standard bus. The smaller Otter chassis catered for medium-capacity requirements with either a Guy four-cylinder petrol engine or the Gardner 4LK diesel.

Debuting at the 1950 Commercial Motor Show was Guy's first underfloor-engined chassis – the Arab UF, later called the LUF. This was fitted with Guy's own horizontal engine, which was put into production by Gardner as its HLW. This was later offered under the Warrior name with an alternate Meadows 5.43 litre engine.

The last trolleybus route was Wolverhampton to Dudley, and the very last trolleybus service was undertaken on 5 March 1967 – a source of regret for many. The first motor bus service on the new route the following morning collided with a car in Garrick Street and had to be towed back to the depot – an inauspicious beginning.

The beginning of the era of the trolleybus. A Tillings Stevens TS6, DA 7741 (fleet number 1) stands at the top of Broad Street, ready to start the first ever journey to Wednesfield, with a crowd of interested onlookers.

Wolverhampton's first trolleybus, Tilling-Stevens TS6 DA7741, operating a test run to Wednesfield. It is posed, ready for the return, near the Rookery Lane bridge. The TS6 had a central entrance in its forty-seat Dodson body and a 50 hp motor. The first fare-paying service was on 29 October 1923.

A Tilling-Stevens TS6 turns round in Prince's Square – the terminus for the Wednesfield route, the first stop being outside the Vine Hotel. All the buildings seen here in Broad Street still remain, though pedestrians no longer wander about quite so freely.

A Tilling Stevens TS6 passes the Town Hall in New Street, when the Bushbury service went this way. It was later re-routed along Stafford Street. The bus still has solid tyres, which were later replaced by pneumatic tyres, enabling a speed increase and more comfort for the passengers.

A Tilling-Stevens TS3 motor bus, No. 8, which entered service in 1918, climbs Victoria Street behind a double-decker tram with an overhead pole fitted, which dates the photograph to about 1923. Soon after this Victoria Street was widened with new buildings on the left, not least the imposing art deco frontage of Beatties department store.

The historic Guy BTX trolleybus No. 33, which entered service on 2 December 1926. With a Dodson body, it was the world's first three-axle trolleybus. It is parked outside the Cleveland Road Depot, the first of a long line of Guy passenger vehicles to be bought by the town of their manufacture. Sidney Guy had been Works Manager at the Sunbeam Motor Car Co., but resigned in 1913 to set up his own company in Park Lane, building light commercial vehicles. In 1924 the company began making passenger-carrying vehicles, and in 1926 Guy produced its first trolleybus.

Guy BTX No. 59 was one of seventy-two of the type bought by Wolverhampton, but before this one went into service it was trialled by Nottingham to see if a six-wheel trolleybus was suitable for its routes. It is shown on the Mansfield Road.

Guy BTX No. 49, which entered service in January 1928 and served until September 1938. This was one of a batch of four Dodson-bodied sixty-one seaters with six rather than five-bay bodies, and the first ever low-slung one-step platform.

Guy BTX No. 63 looking slightly the worse for wear after serving from January 1933 to the end of 1944. It has the wartime headlight covers which reduced headlight effectiveness so much and made driving at night so difficult, as there were of course no streetlights during the blackout. Maintenance was minimal during the war years.

In the late 1920s and early 1930s the Sunbeam Motor Car Co. was suffering financially and turned to commercial vehicles as a solution, something it had ignored in the past. To begin with it offered the sixty–seventy-passenger three-axle Sikh motor bus and the twenty-six-passenger four-wheel Pathan, continuing the use of 'tribal' names it had used for its aero-engines. Neither was successful, so it switched to the sunrise industry of trolleybuses and the six-wheel chassis became the Sunbeam MS2 with a Weyman body. An initial four were ordered and are seen here lined up outside Cleveland Road Depot.

Prince's Square was equipped with Europe's first automatic traffic lights in 1927, initially on overhead wires, and then on a central pole as shown here. A Guy BTX approaches from the direction of Victoria Square.

Guy BTX trolleybuses stand outside Cleveland Road Depot, outside of which was a complicated system of overhead wiring that took great skill for a driver to negotiate.

Guy BTX No. 43, delivered in November 1927 and destined to serve for exactly ten years, stands outside the Cleveland Road Depot. It is on the Penn Fields service, which had been converted to trolleybus operation in 1927, the last trams running in March. The turning circle was at the junction of Lea Road and Stubbs Road.

A Guy BTX turning round at the end of Wrottesley Road at the Tettenhall Upper Green Terminus, with a steamroller parked just off the main road.

A busy Queen Square in the late 1920s with Guy double-deckers plying their routes. To the left a delivery van has its rear doors open outside J. Lyons & Co., delivering bread and cakes. In the distance lies St Mark's Church, always a landmark at the bottom of Darlington Street.

A Sunbeam MS2 with Beadle bodywork, No. 214 is given a tilt test inside the Sunbeam Works in August 1934. Cyril Dabbs, the chief engineer, stands on the extreme left. The bus behind is for an export order to South Africa.

A wartime photograph of Guy BTX No. 79 on the Bushbury Lane 9A service, illustrating how, in several places, passengers had to disembark on the 'wrong' side of the trolleybuses. This bus was scrapped in 1945.

The inaugural 7A service to Darlaston in May 1929 was an extension of the Bilston 7 route, though this Guy BTX, No. 60, is displaying the number 1 to signify that it is the first ever service, and is about to make the trip back to Wolverhampton.

A Guy BT trolleybus with a Park Royal body stands in Victoria Street post-war, waiting to start the 2 service. Park Royal was a north-west London coachbuilder which provided the bodywork for a high proportion of Wolverhampton's buses.

Guy BTX UK 6357 (fleet number 57) is seen standing at the terminus of the Bushbury Hill service, which was at the junction of Old Fallings Lane and Leacroft Avenue. This bus was one of a batch of five delivered on 4 May 1929 and survived in service until 30 September 1938.

A Sunbeam F4 starts the climb up Tettenhall Rock having just passed Tettenhall and Newbridge Garage (now Majestic Wine), behind which is Tettenhall station, which now hosts Wolverhampton's transport museum, the Tettenhall Transport Heritage Centre.

The top of Stafford Street with a Guy trolleybus having just turned from the Cannock Road by the Elephant and Castle pub. Everything in this photograph is now gone, having been demolished to make the road a dual carriageway.

A Guy BTX trolleybus negotiates the small island which used to lie at the bottom of Queen Square, turning out of Victoria Street, with the Hippodrome in front. This was No. 81, a Guy-bodied vehicle with the more aesthetically pleasing flat-fronted design than the early Dodson bodies.

Guy FC single-decker motor bus No. 73 climbs out of Bridgnorth up the Hermitage Hill. It was one of two of these thirty-five seaters purchased in 1928 to operate this route, which had been bought from GWR. It served until 1937.

Guy CX No. 64, with the enclosed staircase of production CX buses, operates by the Prince Albert Pub in Railway Drive.

Guy Motors' bus erection shop in the Park Lane factory, with Warrior single-deck bodies being made in house.

A Guy Warrior overhead maintenance truck outside Cleveland Road Depot, hitched to a Sunbeam which was being retired.

Guy BTX No. 84 with very battered Dodson bodywork negotiates the reversing corner in Bilston, looking the worse for wear. During the war minor damage like that shown here was often not repaired because of a lack of manpower resources. The bus also displays a generally unkempt appearance.

Guy BTX No. 89, which served from 31 March 1933 to 28 May 1947, stands in Railway Drive, ready to make the journey to Penn. The BTX buses, from the prototype onwards, mostly had Dodson bodywork, at least until 1934. Charles Dodson was a Leeds coachbuilder and produced a rather unattractive body for the BTX. A few early BTXs had Guy's own bodies, and after 1934 a number of different coachbuilders were used.

During the war twelve Bournemouth Sunbeam MS2s were loaned to Wolverhampton, still retaining their yellow paintwork with maroon stripes, because of the lack of demand in seaside towns. Here No. 187 negotiates Prince's Square on a snowy day in the bitter winter of 1946/7. As can be seen, the Bournemouth MS2s had two entrances, but in service in Wolverhampton the front door was kept closed, and the poor clippie had to withstand the cold well wrapped up on the open rear platform.

Bournemouth Sunbeam MS2 BEL 814 (No. 129), parked at the Pear Tree terminus. The route ended here because this marked the Borough boundary. This MS2 arrived from Bournemouth on 28 October 1940, and did not return until 7 December 1948, having been thoroughly overhauled and re-painted.

Post-war, Sunbeam W4 No. 443 stands at the same spot as the MS2 in the previous photograph, on route 12A. This bus came into service in March 1947 as one of a large number of Sunbeam W4s ordered to replace the town's motley collection of pre-war, utilitarian wartime and borrowed buses.

A Guy BTX, No. 228, with wartime shrouded headlights, looking weary and worn. This was one of a batch of four BTXs with Brush bodywork that were delivered in 1935, and 228 survived in service until 25 March 1949.

The Guy BTX that followed the bus in the previous photograph off the production line stands in Victoria Square, ready to take the Penn Fields service in December 1935. Victoria Square was a central hub and passenger loading was in the centre of the square.

The first ever Sunbeam, with Weyman bodywork, on the way into town from Tettenhall, even though the destination board has not been changed. It passes the end of Paget Road, looking strangely blank without any adverts, probably because it has only just entered service.

The first ever trolleybus built by Sunbeam, No. 95, posed at the terminus in Tettenhall, alongside the much-missed 'Swiss Chalet' bus shelter, which had been erected in West Park for the Arts & Industrial Exhibition in 1902.

A Guy Arab motor bus among three trolleybuses in a typical post-war Lichfield Street scene. Lichfield Street is once more mainly used by buses, as private cars are now banned, but this may soon change as pedestrianisation plans are being considered at the time of writing.

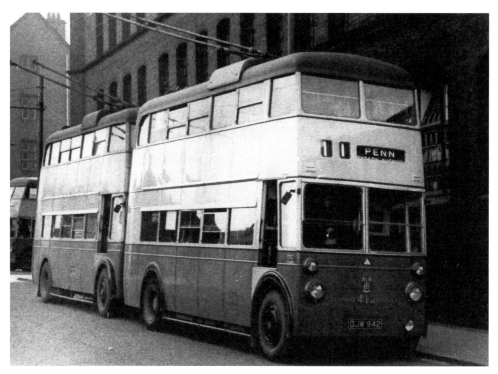

Sunbeam W4 No. 412, delivered in May 1945, is seen parked next to the Chubb building, ready to undertake the 11 service to Penn. The W4 was a wartime utility design built as a combined Sunbeam/Karrier, the sole permitted manufacturer during the war. Over 200 were built, with a timber-framed bodywork.

A line-up of Sunbeam trolleybuses outside the Cleveland Road Depot, with four single-deck MF1s in the foreground and four double-deck MS2s behind. The first one in the row is No. 206, an MF1 that entered service on 30 March 1934 and served until 24 March 1945. Over 120 MF1/2/3s were built between 1934 and 1942, and over 500 MS2s.

Guy BTX No. 82 with a Guy body, which entered service in November 1931 and served until April 1946. What looks like an enthusiast with a camera suggests it is probably just post-war.

A Guy BTX which entered service in March 1931 and soldiered on until the end of May 1945, looking worn during the war with the headlights still masked. Of course, during the war the interior lighting also had to be severely dimmed, which made conductors' tasks harder, as well as the drivers'.

A Dodson-bodied GUY BTX, No. 83, the first of a batch of nine which began to be delivered in June 1932. The cab roofs on these looked far less basic than the early BTXs, but the space over the cab was yet to be exploited to fit four more passengers.

An early BTX standing at the Prince's Square traffic lights in Lichfield Street on the 1 service from Tettenhall.

One of the first production batch of Guy BTX double-decker trolleybuses, No. 37, delivered on 11 February 1927, is seen standing in Lichfield Street while on the Penn Fields service.

A Tilling-Stevens TS6, No. 22, having been refitted with pneumatic tyres, which, apart from the better ride quality, from 1 October 1928, increased the permitted top speed from 12 mph to 20 mph. This was increased yet again on 1 January 1931, to 30 mph. This bus was operating the Fordhouses service, the terminus at the Vine being one of fifteen throughout Wolverhampton.

A Henry Meadows 6DC630 diesel engine, fitted to a small number of the buses made by Meadows's neighbour in Fallings Park, Guy Motors. Wolverhampton Corporation generally preferred Gardner diesels.

The advert on this Sunbeam W4 trolleybus, No. 449, dates the photograph well, as 'Drinka pinta milka day' is well remembered from the mid-1960s, just at the time where the trolleybuses were being phased out in favour of an all-motor bus fleet. Symbolically, the Guy Arab IV full-fronted motor bus in the new experimental, predominantly green colours, lurks behind.

Two Guy BT trolleybuses wait at the terminus in St James Square. No. 635 in the foreground is about to make the 29 service to Walsall, and No. 638 behind is on the short service route to Willenhall. This is *c.* 1963, when coal merchants were still advertising on buses – not something you see today, or Wolverhampton Steam Laundry for that matter.

Another Guy BT trolleybus waiting to make the No. 29 service to Walsall from St James Square, which is a square which is no longer there after the redevelopment of Horseley Fields. This bus, fleet no. 498, served from 1949 to 1965.

A Sunbeam W4, No. 452, passes along Cannock Road at the end of Cambridge Street on 15 September 1963. Apart from the trolleybus wires, much of this scene still remains, though the Coach and Horses pub, which is out of sight to the right, is no longer there, having been replaced by a Polish supermarket.

A Guy BT stands outside the long-lamented Elephant & Castle pub on Stafford Street, at the end of the Cannock Road. Nothing in this scene is still there, the pub becoming a grass patch after being demolished by developers just before it was to be listed, with a shopping centre built behind it. The Black Country Living Museum has a plan to build a replica of the Elephant & Castle, with its wonderful tiled frontage.

The end is nigh, as two Guy BTs, Nos 494 and 645, await scrapping, along with a Guy Arab III single-decker, FJW 565, at the rear of Park Lane Depot *c.* 1967.

Four Guy BTs, Nos 459, 490, 437, 441, awaiting scrapping in March 1967. Strangely, they are in Don Everall's yard in Monmore Green.

A last act of defiance – the overhead wires brought down by Sunbeam W4 DJW 904 on its last ever run being positioned on the scrapping line at Park Lane Depot in June 1963.

Motor Buses

Though the green and yellow municipal buses were the most common sight on Wolverhampton's streets, private bus companies also operated into the town, including the famous Midland Red. In the 1970s Warstones Motors started a bus operation which became the much-loved Green Bus Company. The first route was actually Cannock to Penkridge, with a Leyland Olympian and a Bedford single-decker as the first equipment. With its depot in Great Wyrley, the company became a familiar sight in the villages to the north and east of Wolverhampton, with services from Brewood, Wheaton Aston, Blymhill and the like to Telford and Wolverhampton. A Guy Arab became its first double-decker, and it was known for its eclectic mix of well-maintained vehicles operating to out-of-the-way places.

Guy Motors entered the 1960s with a revolutionary new motor bus: the Wulfrunian. Surprisingly, it had a vertically mounted front Gardner 6LX engine together with a front entrance. It had full air suspension and disc brakes. It was largely designed to the requirement of West Riding, which was to be its main customer. Only 137 Wulfrunians were built, mostly going to West Riding, though two demonstrators were trialled by Wolverhampton and many other bus operators.

The failure of the Wulfrunian had a dire financial effect on Guy, which was taken over by Jaguar in October 1961. The last trolleybus was about to be made, for Bournemouth, and after the demise of the Wulfrunian in 1962 the Arab was updated as the Arab V, which could be fitted with front or rear-entrance bodywork. In 1966 Jaguar/Guy was taken over by the British Motor Corporation, which in turn became part of Leyland in 1968. The following year the Arab was discontinued, and for the first time in over fifty years Wolverhampton no longer made buses.

After the disappearance of the trolleybuses, the corporation's transport department did not have long left to exist itself. In 1969 it was taken over by the West Midlands Passenger Transport Executive (WMPTE), along with the public transport services of Birmingham, Walsall and West Bromwich. WMPTE had been set up to govern the bus services of the West Midlands, and had a total of 2,100 buses and 8,500 employees. The buses continued to operate in their original colours until such time as they were repainted, after which they emerged in the cream and blue PTE colours, which were based on the Birmingham colours. Route numbers were changed, with Wolverhampton's old numbers being replaced in a new 500 series, so that the premier route 1 to Tettenhall became 501.

Later on, the bus services of Coventry were also incorporated, and as the private Midland Red Company operated many services in the West Midlands an agreement was reached in December 1973 for WMPTE to purchase those routes that lay wholly within its area, raising the number of buses in the fleet to 2,600.

Much of the Wolverhampton fleet was in poor condition, and it was not long before the vehicles were being replaced by rear-engined, driver-operated Daimler Fleetlines.

After the Transport Act of 1985, which deregulated bus services, the actual operation of the bus service and its assets was transferred to a separate legal entity, West Midlands Travel Ltd, which remained in public ownership until sold to its management and employees in 1991. Subsequently, the company was bought by National Express.

In August 1993 a Volvo B10L single-decker, 1469, had an alarming accident on the Broad Street Bridge, on the Wednesfield route. It swung off the road and was left hanging half over the canal, leaving a scene reminiscent of something from *The Italian Job*. Fortunately, the driver and all the passengers were able to safely disembark at the rear. When the breakdown team were informed that a bus needed towing on the bridge, they asked which way it was facing so they could arrive in the most convenient direction for towing it. They were puzzled when they were told it did not matter which way they came, but saw the explanation as soon as they arrived.

WMPTE was responsible for the reintroduction of trams to the West Midlands. Discussions aimed at returning trams to the area had taken place several times since the war, but began in earnest in 1988. There was a grand proposal to build three lines linking Birmingham, Wolverhampton, Walsall, Birmingham Airport, Chelmsley Wood and the Merry Hill Shopping Centre, and the towns in between. The first line between the centres of Wolverhampton and Birmingham, passing along old redundant rail lines for much of its route, was not begun until 1995 and this solitary Midland Metro line opened on 30 May 1999. Twenty years later, apart from an extension from Snow Hill to New Street in Birmingham, and from Bilston Street to the railway station in Wolverhampton, it remains the only one.

It was initially operated by sixteen Italian Ansaldobreda T69 156 passenger trams from a depot in Wednesbury, but these were replaced in 2004–5 by twenty-one Spanish CAF Urbo-3 210 passenger trams. More an inter-city service than a suburban tram system, like the old Lorain trams, the Midland Metro carries 6 million people annually. Further lines and extensions are still planned.

As National Express West Midlands the bus fleet adopted a red and white colour scheme, with red to the front. More recently single-colour route-signalled paintwork has been adopted using colours such as crimson and platinum. Another innovation was giving many of the 1,600 buses now in service girls' names. Meanwhile, electric power returned to the streets of Wolverhampton, albeit in the form of hybrid power, as a large fleet of Alexander-Dennis Enviro 400 double-deckers was introduced. The route numbering was also adapted, and single digit numbers returned to the Wolverhampton streets, though sometimes on longer cross-town routes; for instance, the premier 1 route goes directly from Dudley through Sedgley and Wolverhampton to Tettenhall.

Guy Motors concentrated on truck production after the Arab line was closed (and the Warrior not long afterwards) and was one of the few divisions of Leyland to be making a profit when it was closed down in 1982 as it was competing with other divisions. After the pioneering work of ECC, Guy and Sunbeam, it was a sad day.

The streets of Wolverhampton are now filled with not just National Express buses, but those of many other private companies, like Arriva, Travel Express, iGo, Let's Go, Select, Diamond and Banga Travel. They operate from a new bus station over the ring road from the railway station, with, at the time of writing, a Metro extension being built down Piper's Row to create a transport interchange.

In the 1920s and 1930s days out in a charabanc became popular, a charabanc commonly being a bus with light bodywork and a folding roof, which would later be called a coach. This is a small charabanc with a Wolverhampton registration, about to take a group of Heath Town residents on an outing from outside a barber's shop.

A charabanc of Tours & Transport of King Street, an early operator, about to start an outing from outside Hilton Hall, Featherstone.

Children of St Luke's School in Blakenhall line up on the playground, ready to board Don Everall coaches for an outing, just after the Second World War.

A Guy coach, XUK 768, posed outside the Pigot Arms in Pattingham. This is a Warrior forty-one-seat chassis with futuristic Burlingham bodywork, believed to be one of only two such vehicles. The fact that the side of the coach features the Guy Indian headdress symbol suggests this is a company publicity photograph rather than a vehicle in service with a local operator.

A Daimler coach on the Don Everall inspection ramp, with two AECs behind. The Don Everall coach depot was in Monmore Green, off Bilston Road.

A Commer with a Duple body, RUK 846, on the inspection ramp in the Don Everall yard in Monmore Green.

A line-up of eleven new Don Everall forty-one-seat Beadle-Commer TS3 coaches. Beadle was a Dartford coachwork builder. They are lined up in the Monmore Green Depot; Don Everall also had depots in West Bromwich and Stourbridge.

Don Everall provided the coach for the Wolves team's away trips, with the driver having his own dedicated blazer badge. They also supplied this coach for an open-top bus tour of the town in 1960, parading the FA Cup. They are just arriving for a civic reception at the Town Hall, with crowds of fans filling Cheapside.

The Don Everall depot in Monmore Green with Guy Arab buses and various coaches to be seen. In the background is the solitary cooling tower of the Commercial Road Power Station. The site was fronted by Don Everall's Ford car dealership on the Bilston Road.

A Wolverhampton Corporation Daimler which attempted to pass underneath the Town Hall in the High Street, Bridgnorth, on 16 May 1949. The High Street is one-way these days, and no vehicles are allowed to drive underneath the Town Hall.

An AEC Reliance single-decker with Park Royal bodywork, No. 707 was one of three such buses to enter service in 1964 on country routes. It waits at the Railway Drive bus station to undertake the 16 service to Pattingham.

A Guy Arab, now in WMPTE colours, ascends Darlington Street on its way from Tettenhall.

A 1957-delivered Guy Arab III, SUK 11, passes a 1959-delivered Guy Arab IV, YDA 33, with full frontal bodywork, on the Bilston Road. The full frontal design was not liked by fitters as engine access was difficult.

A Guy Arab IV, YDA 30, in the experimental green colour scheme with only a narrow yellow band, works its way down Pipers Row. Wolverhampton Steam Laundry is still being advertised on the front, but as a sign of the times the revolutionary pedestrianised Mander Shopping Centre is featured on the side.

A one-man operated single-decker Daimler Roadliner, NJW 718E, stands in the Railway Drive bus station waiting to make the journey on the 36 service to Wombourne. The six Roadliners purchased had the same poor-quality Strachan bodies as six AEC Swifts, and both types suffered as a result. Note the Wolverhampton Corporation Transport Department had come down on the side of those who insist the village should be spelled without the 'E' for their destination blinds.

A Green Bus Company Leyland Titan PD3, MJA 892G, new in 1969 and ex-Stockport. It was bought by the Green Bus Co. in 1982 and is shown in Chubb Street in October 1984.

A Midland Red Daimler Fleetline, TRE 949L, which was once operated by Harper Bros of Cannock, which was bought out by Midland Red. It is shown in Railway Drive. Fleetlines came out in 1960, the second major rear-engined double-deckers after the Leyland Atlantean.

A Midland Red, Chaserider-branded Daimler Fleetline, SMA 858G (No. 6158), at the bus station in September 1984. When WMPTE acquired Midland Red's West Midlands routes they had a combined fleet of 2,100 Fleetlines.

A Midland Red Leyland National, NOE 595R, operated by Midland Red's Chaserider brand, in the bus station in 1984, with the derelict Queens Building in the background looking lost and forlorn, and in imminent danger of demolition. Thankfully it was saved and put to good use as the centrepiece of the development of the new transport hub. Over 7,000 Leyland Nationals were built between 1972 and 1985.

A Midland Red mid-engined Leyland Leopard, JHA 234L, built in 1973, is seen standing at the bus station in September 1984. The buildings in the background, including the Little Swan pub, are at the top of Horseley Fields and were about to be demolished.

A Chase Bus Services Leyland National, HJA 127N, at the bus station in 1988, alongside Daimler Fleetline NOC 436R (No. 6436), which was later sold to Amberline of Liverpool, These two buses had become the main types offered by British Leyland at the time, replacing an assortment of different brands which the conglomerate had acquired.

The second of two Guy Wulfrunians, 4071 FJW, was trialled by Wolverhampton and is seen standing at the stop at Fighting Cocks. These were the first buses with air suspension and disc brakes, but suffered from being front-engined, meaning the entrance was behind the front wheels and therefore the driver, making single-man operation difficult.

The transport department's Bilston Street yard with a variety of Guy Arabs, in both traditional yellow and green and the experimental mostly green colours, with the nose of the first Guy Wulfrunian poking forward, *c.* 1970. This Wulfrunian had six fewer seats then the second one trialled by Wolverhampton.

The old toast-rack style bus station in 1988, with, of course, someone running for a bus, either one of the two Fleetlines or maybe the Leyland National.

A Bristol VR, No. 4685, being followed closely by another and a Metrobus in the old 'toast-rack' style bus station in August 1974. The Metro-Cammell-Weymann Metrobus was built from 1977 to 1989, and WMPTE had a fleet of over 1,100.

A Foden recovery vehicle, No. 105, about to tow a Daimler Fleetline in Fryer Street. A Leyland National and another Fleetline are stuck behind them, and the end of Short Street is also blocked.

A Daimler Fleetline, SDA 785S, at the side of Park Lane Depot on 14 April 1984. The Guy factory is in the background on the other side of Park Lane.

Daimler Fleetline No. 6677 is seen standing at the drop-off point at the end of the old bus station with the old Victoria Hotel, now the Britannia Hotel, in the background.

One of a number of
Wolverhampton buses
recycled into use as a playbus
for Wolverhampton Young
Volunteers, based on the Dudley
Road, this is Guy Arab SUK 3.

An interesting collection of buses in the bus station in October 1988, featuring from the left: a
WMPTE Metrobus and Daimler Fleetline, a Midland Red Leyland Leopard, a WMPTE Fleetline,
a Midland Red Metrobus and another WMPTE Metrobus.

At a time when Wulfruna Street had a significant number of bus termini, three Daimler Fleetlines resplendent in their WMPTE colours and featuring Wolverhampton's new route numbers in the '500' series wait to start their journeys, including No. 559 to Ashmore Park via Wednesfield. The brick and concrete 'bunker' of the Civic Centre looms in the background.

A National Express West Midlands Volvo B7RLE single-decker, No. 2013, named *Sonia*, enters Chapel Ash from Merridale Road on the cross-city route-branded service to Fordhouses and Springhill, featuring the new mono colour scheme, all red in this case.

An Alexander-Dennis Enviro 400 hybrid enters Chapel Ash from Tettenhall on the long route 1, which will terminate in Dudley. The first photo in this book features a horse-drawn tram on this very spot.

Two National Express West Midlands Volvo B7RLE single-deckers negotiate Prince's Square where once Tilling Stevens single-decker trolleybuses terminated. The one turning out of Broad Street is SN5 LCF (No. 2024).

An Arriva service to Cannock moves along Stafford Street. A VDLSB200, YJ61 FEP (No. 3762) is normally based in the Cannock Depot. VDL is a Dutch company and took over the DAF bus business.

A Volvo B7RLE, BX61 LKL, on the 25 service passes through Bilston. The name *Helga Marie* graces this bus.

In a scene reminiscent of the end of the film *The Italian Job*, a WMPTE Volvo B10L single-decker, R469 XDA (No. 1469), crashed through the parapet of the Broad Street bridge and hung precariously over the canal. The driver and passengers escaped unharmed through the rear. This bus has now been scrapped.

Tram rails being re-laid once more in Wolverhampton: the Midland Metro rails going down on 4 October 1997 at the end of the Bilston Road, forming the initial Wolverhampton terminus of the 1 route.

An AnsaldoBreda T-69 stands waiting at the Bilston Street terminus of the Midland Metro line 1 in 1999. Sixteen of these trams began the service on 27 April 1999, but they were replaced by twenty Spanish CAF Urbo 3s in 2014.

The Queen's Building. Opened in 1849 as the ticket offices and HQ of the London & North Western Railway, it formed the gateway to the approach to High Level station until the road was realigned in the 1880s, and the archways were filled in. It is one of the oldest railway buildings in the Black Country and now is a landmark for the adjacent transport hub, housing a cafe, with the new bus station alongside and High Level station being re-developed, with the Midland Metro tram tracks running by.

The Piper's Row entrance to the new bus station with Volvo single-decker BX61 XBK (No. 2064) and Dennis Trident 2 BX02 AUU (No. 4344) in the background, as well as a new Platinum Alexander-Dennis Enviro in the foreground. It would be interesting to know if the original Stan & Ollie (Hardy) were advertised on buses in the 1930s.

Two Alexander-Dennis Enviro 400 hybrids pass along Piper's Row by the bus station, No. 5401 *Abigail* going towards Victoria Square and No. 5413 *Libby June* going the other way. The Midland Metro tram tracks are in the road, but the trams had not yet started running from Bilston Street as work was still underway, hence the barriers and cones.

A Dennis Dart SLF of Travel Express, Y854 TGH, with a Plaxton body, turns off Stafford Street into the Cannock Road on the 11 service to Underhill. The National Express bus behind is not chasing the same passengers as it is 'Not in service'.

An Arriva service to Perton leaves the new bus station on the dedicated bus lane next to the ring road, which will allow it to pass up Broad Street and back through the city centre without turning on to the ring road.

A Midland Metro CAF Urbo 3 tram approaches the ring road roundabout on the Bilston Road. The clear view of the old Royal Hospital in the background resulted from the demolition of the Cleveland Road Wolverhampton Municipal Tramways Car Depot, which would have previously obscured it.

The Midland Metro Bilston Street terminus, half turned into a bus terminus prior to the tram tracks down Piper's Row being opened. A Banga Travel Optare Solo stands at the old Metro platform, while a red Enviro 400, No. 5410 *Jade* from Tettenhall Wood, and a single-decker Alexander-Dennis E20D, YY14 WHC (No. 753), stand in front of the Bilston Street Police Station.

A preserved Sunbeam W4 with Charles Roe bodywork, which served as fleet number 433 from June 1946 to 6 March 1967, when it was stored for preservation by the Science Museum after restoration by the Wolverhampton Trolleybus Group. It later passed to the Black Country Living Museum, where it operates on the museum's on-site network. Here it is shown at the Steam & Vintage Rally in West Park.

The ornate tiled Municipal Tramways Car Depot sign inside the Cleveland Road Municipal Tramways Car Depot, which was demolished in 2017. Efforts to save the sign for use in the new Black Country Living Museum Tram Depot were thwarted when the demolition contractors smashed it.

Preserved AEC Regal III coach CFK 340, which used to be operated by Burnham's of Worcester, is seen operating an enthusiasts' service along Wolverhampton's routes – Oxbarn Avenue being displayed on the destination roll in front. It has stopped at Wolverhampton's transport museum at Tettenhall station, and is a reminder that Wolverhampton Corporation operated three AEC Reliances and five AEC Renowns post-war.

Renowned bus enthusiast and historian Don Phipps is seen driving Wolverhampton tram No. 49 in the Black Country Living Museum. Built as a Lorain system tram, this was converted to overhead collection.

Guy BTX trolleybus UK 9978 (No. 78) in storage in the Black Country Living Museum awaiting restoration. It is shown on 25 May 2003, but remains much the same today.